THE ISLE OF WIGHT
COAST PATH

by
JOHN N. MERRILL

Maps and photographs by John N. Merrill.

a J.N.M. PUBLICATION

1990

a J.N.M. PUBLICATION,

J.N.M. PUBLICATIONS,
WINSTER,
MATLOCK,
DERBYSHIRE.
DE4 2DQ
☎ *Winster (062988) 454*
Fax: Winster (062988) 416

Conceived, edited, typeset, designed, paged, marketed and distributed by John N. Merrill.

© Text and Routes - John N. Merrill 1990.

© Maps and photographs - John N. Merrill 1990.

First Published -   January 1988
Reprinted - August 1990.

ISBN 0 907496 68 7

Meticulous research has been undertaken to ensure that this publication is highly accurate at the time of going to press. The publishers, however, cannot be held responsible for alterations, errors or omissions, but they would welcome notification of such for future editions.

Typeset in - Plantin - bold, italic and plain 9pt and 18pt.

Printed by - Commercial Colour Press, London. E7 0EW

Cover Sketch - Culver Down and Sandwood Bsy - by John Creber © J.N.M. PUBLICATIONS 1990.

An all British product.

ABOUT
JOHN N. MERRILL

John combines the characteristics and strength of a mountain climber with the stamina and athletic capabilities of a marathon runner. In this respect he is unique and has to his credit a whole string of remarkable long walks. He is without question the world's leading marathon walker.

Over the last fifteen years he has walked more than 100,000 miles and successfully completed ten walks of a least 1,000 miles or more. His six major walks in Great Britain are -

Hebridean Journey........ 1,003 miles.
Northern Isles Journey......913 miles.
Irish Island Journey ....1,578 miles.
Parkland Journey........2,043 miles.
Land's End to John o' Groats.....1,608 miles.

and in 1978 he became the first person (permanent Guinness Book of Records entry) to walk the entire coastline of Britain - 6,824 miles in ten months.

In Europe he has walked across Austria - 712 miles - hiked the Tour of Mont Blanc, completed High Level Routes in the Dolomites and Italian Alps, and the GR20 route across Corsica in training! In 1982 he walked across Europe - 2,806 miles in 107 days - crossing seven countries, the Swiss and French Alps and the complete Pyrennean chain - the hardest and longest mountain walk in Europe, with more than 600,000 feet of ascent!

In America he used The Appalachian Trail - 2,200 miles - as a training walk, He has walked from Mexico to Canada via the Pacific Crest Trail in record time - 118 days for 2,700 miles. He has walked most of the Continental Divide Trail and much of New Mexico; his second home. In Canada he has walked the Rideau Trail - Kingston to Ottowa - 220 miles and The Bruce Trail - Tobermory to Niagara Falls - 460 miles.

In 1984 John set off from Virginia Beach on the Atlantic coast, and walked 4,226 miles without a rest day, across the width of America to Santa Cruz and San Francisco on the Pacific coast. His walk is unquestionably his greatest achievement, being, in modern history, the longest, hardest crossing of the U.S.A. in the shortest time - under six months (178 days). The direct distance is 2,800 miles.

Between major walks John is out training in his own area - The Peak District National Park. He has walked all of our National Trails many times - The Cleveland Way thirteen times and The Pennine Way four times in a year! He has been trekking in the Himalayas five times. He created more than a dozen challenge walks which have been used to raise more than £250,000 for charity. From his own walks he has raised over £100,000. He is author of more than one hundred walking guides; most of which he publishes himself, His book sales are in excess of 2 1/2 million, He has created many long distance walks including The Limey Way , The Peakland Way, Dark Peak Challenge walk, and Rivers' Way. He lectures extensively in Britain and America.

CONTENTS

ROYAL YATCH SQUADRON CLUB HOUSE, COWES

YARMOUTH

FISHERMAN'S COTTAGE INN, SHANKLIN

INTRODUCTION

Coastal walking has always held a deep fascination for me. I never tire of seeing the sea in all all its moods, from placid tranquil scenes of almost apologetic waves to the awesome power of seas whipped up by galeforce winds. Walking along the shore you see different wildlife from on land, making a delightful contrast. Coastal walking is not easy, for there are many ups and downs and twists and turns along the way, but it all makes rewarding walking.

My love of coastal walking started on the islands of The Hebrides and spread to the Northern Isles, Ireland and in 1978 by my walk around the British shoreline. In 1980 I was asked to join a party walking the Isle of Wight coast path but because of work commitments I couldn't make it. I was also not ready mentally after my British walk to walk along the shore again. I am glad that the idea of walking the Isle of Wight remained on file and by 1987 I was ready to see for myself what it was like.

Like all my walks I went with no preconceived ideas, preferring to learn about the area and see it afresh. The end result is an exceptional walk around an incredibly varied coastline. In fact I doubt whether any other short coastal walk could encompass such variety. I set off from Ryde in blistering heat, experienced soft rain around The Needles, and more matchless weather along the northern shore back to Ryde. In view of the 1987 summer, I had been lucky.

The book then descibes and details my walk around the Isle of Wight Coast Path, with details of where to stay or camp, walking instructions, maps and some of the photographs I took along the way. For a very pleasant week's walk around an island I cannot think of a finer circuit. I hope the sun shines every day for you and that you enjoy it as much as I did.

HAPPY WALKING!

John N. Merrill.

JOHN N. MERRILL.

ABOUT THE WALK -

MAP — The whole walk is covered by the O.S. 1:25,000 Outdoor Leisure Map No 29 — Isle of Wight.

There is no time limit to the walk and you can walk it in stages or over several days. It is simply a matter of going out and enjoying yourself. You can have a central base and walk sections of it; stay in hotels or bed and breakfast establishments as you walk round; or backpack and use a campsite every night. As you can see from the Amenities Guide there is ample scope. The two "lonely" sections where there are no facilities are from Blackgang to Freshwater Bay on the south western side of the island, and around the Hamstead peninsula on the north western side.

I have based the walk starting from Ryde — the Gateway to the Island — but you can start it where ever you like depending on your arrival point. I walked it in four days (96 hours), arriving mid afternoon in Ryde and walking to St. Helen's. Day 2 to St. Catherine's (Niton). Day 3 to Totland, before The Needles. Day 4 to Great Thorness and the last half day to Ryde. Although it is said to be approximately 60 miles round, I can assure you it is 77 miles as I have detailed.

The Isle of Wight County Council have created the coast walk but differs slightly from mine near Luccombe to St. Lawrence, following the original route through the Landslip; scenicly one of the finest parts of the island. I believe coastal walking is walking the nearest right of way to the sea. At several places there are coast path signs — blue with white lettering. Accomodation is generally open all year but some campsites are only open between Easter and September. The County Council produce four leaflets detailing the coast path and the Tourist Office in Ryde has lists of accomodation and campsite information.

Starting from Ryde you have a mixture of shore and road walking to St. Helen's but a pleasant starter to the walk. Next you walk around Bembridge to the impressive White Cliffs and Culver Down before reaching the seaside resorts of Sandown, Shanklin and Ventnor. After this it is back to the cliffs and inland slightly to Niton and St. Catherine's. The cliffs from here to near Freshwater Bay are mostly soft with frequent large landslips and considerable erosion. At Freshwater Bay they become more stable, leading to the dramatic chalk creations of The Needles. Now on the north western side of the island you cross heather downs and return to the shoreline to gain Yarmouth. Beyond you walk around the Hamstead Penisula, walking far inland to walk around the Newtown River estuary. After the fascinating village of Newtown you begin making for the shore at Thorness Bay and the sea is your companion all the way to Cowes. Here you cross the River Medina by ferry and road walk to Wooton Bridge. Here you are on the last lap as you weave your way inland back to Ryde, completing your circuit.

A master record of people who have walked the route using this guidebook is kept by John Merrill at J.N.M Publications. Those who complete the walk are eligible for a a special four colour embroidered badge and signed certificate from J.N.M. Publications.

Useful address — The Isle of Wight County Council, County Hall, Newport, Isle of Wight. PO31 1UD.

VENTNOR BAY

ABOUT THE ISLAND -

Created during the Victorian period as a holiday isle because of its mild climate, the island is diamond shaped being 23½ miles wide — from Culver Down to The Needles — and 13¾ miles wide — from Cowes to St. Catherine's Point. The northern side, facing the mainland, is often referred to as the 'front' of the island. The main river, the Medina, flows north to Cowes and divides the island with the main resorts and population on the eastern side. The island was originally the southern wall of the River Solent. The sea gradually eroded the valley side down and eventually flooded the valley.

The highest point is St. Boniface Down at 785 feet and part of one of the islands major down systems. The other to the north reaches a height of 700 feet. The south western coast, often referred to as the 'back of the island', is an area of considerable erosion due to the clay formation. East of St. Catherine's Point, the southernmost tip of the island, is The Undercliff. Here the cliff has slipped anything upto ½ mile inland forming cliffs as high as 150 feet.

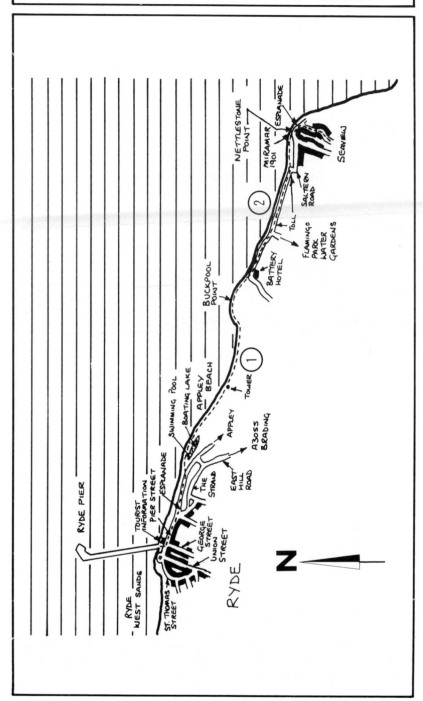

RYDE TO SEAVIEW (NETTLESTONE POINT) — 2½ MILES
- allow one hour.

ABOUT THE SECTION — Leaving Ryde you keep close to coastline, first along a road then along a walkway with Ryde East Sands and Appley Beach beside you. Little over a mile, at Puckpool Point, you return to road walking, still beside the sands, to reach Nettlestone Point at Seaview. A very pleasant curtain raiser to the north eastern side of the island.

WALKING INSTRUCTIONS — Facing the railway station and pier, turn right — heading eastwards — along Pier Street and Esplanade, passing Ryde Castle Hotel, Bowling Green, and Seacrest Hotel. Here leave the road and keep to the left to pass the boating lake on your right to gain the walkway around Appley Beach. Keeping the beach on your left follow the walkway past the imposing Appley Tower and around Puckpool Point to gain the road at Spring Vale, close to the Battery Hotel. Continue ahead on the road, with the shore on your left. ¼ mile later keep ahead on the toll road, and just over ¼ mile later at the other toll entrance at Saltern Road keep ahead on the path to reach Nettlestone Point, Miramar dated 1901, and the Esplanade at Sea View. Follow the road for a few yards to where it turns sharp right and ascends into the main village of Seaview.

RYDE — The "Gateway to the Island." The pier was built in 1813 and is the second longest in England, after Southend's. The town was once a fishing village but, like much of the island, became a major holiday resort in Victorian times. The town is now the principal arrival point to the island and in 1965 was the location for the first regular hovercraft service in the world.

RYDE WEST SANDS

5

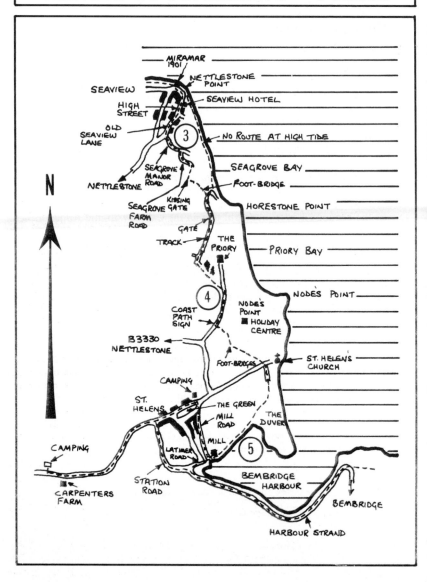

THE DUVER — Former site of the Isle of Wight golf course, but now protected by the National Trust. The area is extraordinarily rich in wild flowers and more than 260 species have been recorded.

ST. HELEN'S MILL — The mill's ponds on the western side of the harbour were tidal and used to store water at high tide, which was used to feed the waterwheel of the mill.

SEAVIEW TO ST. HELENS (MILL) — 3 MILES - allow 1½ hours.

ABOUT THE SECTION — There are no continuous footpaths close to the shore in this section and you have to ascend away from the sea. The walking is good on pleasant paths through woodland and across fields. Enticing views of the coast are glimpsed before gaining it close to the ruins of St. Helen's Church. From here you walk across the old golf course to the causeway around Bembridge Harbour. At the mill the section ends. Close by are three camp sites; one you passed near St. Helen's Church.

WALKING INSTRUCTIONS — From the junction at Nettlestone Point where the road turns sharp right — High Street — there is a footpath which keeps close to the shore for ½ mile around part of Seagrove Bay. This path is impassable at High Tide, and you will have to walk inland by ascending the High Street of Seaview, past the shops, Bank and Seaview Hotel. Continue along Old Seaview Lane and turn left into the No Through Road, Seagrove Manor Road. A few yards later turn right onto the track of Seagrove Farm Road, also a No Through Road. Follow the track round to your left with football field on your right. A short distance later turn sharp right onto a path and gain a kissing gate. Here you turn left and descend to a footbridge and just after gain Ferniclose Road. To your left is where the coast path comes in and is signed — Seaview ½ mile.

Turn right along Ferniclose Road and soon reach a gate. You now walk along a track, and after ¼ mile it turns sharp left and becomes a beautiful walk underneath fir trees. Well to your left is The Priory and golf course. In another ¼ mile gain a tarmaced lane beside coast path sign — Seaview 1 mile, Bembridge 2 miles. Follow this for 50 yards past the entrance to Nodes Point Holiday Centre and just after on your left is a kissing gate and coast path sign. Descend the field to footbridges before turning left along the lefthand edge of the field to a stile and path sign. Just to your left is a beach and the ruins of St. Helen's Church. On gaining the road here you basically keep straight ahead on the road and walk through the site of the Royal Isle of Wight Golf Links given to the National Trust in 1961. After ¼ mile leave the road and follow the path across the grass to tarmaced causeway, and follow this to the Mill and Latimer Road which leads to the B3395 Bembridge road.

Just before the road by turning right up Mill Road you reach the impressive Green of St. Helens, with a campsite a little to your right and on the other side of The Green. A further campsite at Carpenters Farm, a mile away, is reached by following the B3330 Brading road.

ST. HELEN'S CHURCH — 12th century church of which part of the tower remains, and now used as a seamark. The church was abandoned in the 18th century when the new church was built in 1717.

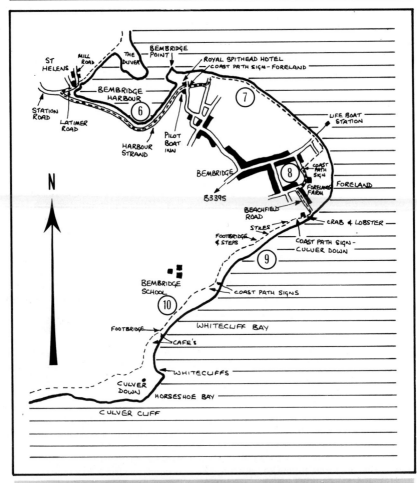

BEMBRIDGE — The harbour is a feeding site for wildfowl and waders. The Spithead Hotel is a reminder to the importance of The Solent and Spithead. Here have been the reviews of the fleet and the gathering of the D-Day armada. The area is also rich in wrecks and was the mooring point for the boats carrying the first settlers to Australia.

ST HELENS (MILL) TO WHITECLIFF BAY (CAFE) — 5 MILES
- allow 2¼ hours.

ABOUT THE SECTION — First you walk round Bembridge Harbour before gaining the shore and walking round to Foreland, the north easterly point of the island. Shortly afterwards you begin ascending along the clifftops as the scenery dramatically changes to the impressive Whitecliffs and bay.

WALKING INSTRUCTIONS — From the Mill walk along Latimer Road to gain the B3395 Bembridge road and turn left along it, walking around Bembridge Harbour to Bembridge Point, a mile away. In the latter stages you walk along Harbour Strand. At the Royal Spithead Hotel, leave the road on the right of it, as coast path signed — Foreland. First along a track and at the end of it turn left then right onto signed path and walk either just inside the trees or along the shoreline for just under a mile to the pier of the Bembridge Lifeboat Station. Continue ahead for a few more yards to a kissing gate. Turn right and follow the fenced path. At the end turn left and right at Forelands Farm. Take the second road on your left — Beachfield Road — and at the end gain the coastline and turn right to the Crab and Lobster Inn. Take the path on the left of the inn close to the cliffs. A few yards later reach the coast path sign — Culver Down. You now keep to the top of the cliffs along a path which is well stiled, signed and with footbridges. You keep on this for 1½ miles, passing Bembridge School on your right before reaching the path down the cliffs to Whitecliff Bay and cafes.

ST. HELENS CHURCH

WHITECLIFF BAY TO SANDOWN — 3½ MILES

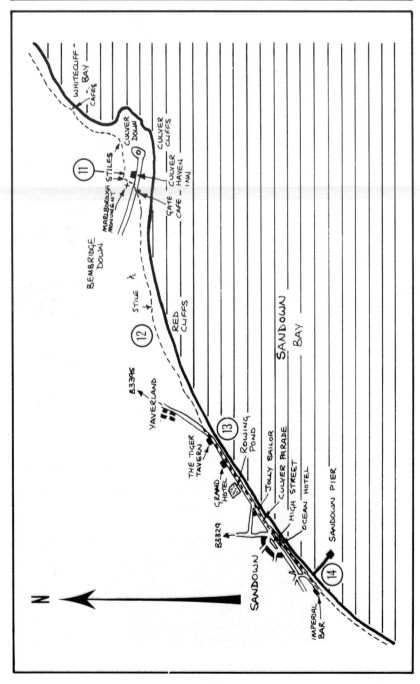

WHITECLIFF BAY TO SANDOWN (PIER) — 3½ MILES
- allow 1½ hours.

ABOUT THE SECTION — A magnificent stretch of coastline with the impressive Whitecliffs before the ascent of Culver Down and its extensive views to the north and south. Next follows a delightful high level walk above the cliffs to the contrasting Red Cliff and the descent to Sandown. One of the finest sections on the whole walk.

WALKING INSTRUCTIONS — From the path junction above Whitecliff Bay Cafe continue along the coast path towards the Whitecliffs. Pass through a stile and ascend the distinct path angling to your right up the slope of Culver Down. Over the next stile, continue ahead to the next and turn left to pass the Yarlborough Monument and Culver Haven Inn. At the road turn right then left almost immediately on the right of a cafe by the gate and begin the gradual descent above the cliffs to Red Cliff a mile away. After these and skirting a Holiday Centre on your right continue descending to the B3395 road at Yaverland. Follow the road past the Tiger Tavern, Grand Hotel and rowing lake into Culver Parade in Sandown. Approaching the High Street, turn left into the Esplanade and follow this to Sandown Pier.

CULVER DOWN — National Trust property reaching a height of 343 feet above the sea. The chalk cliffs are part of the chalk ridge which reappears at The Needles. The monument on top was erected in 1849 in memory of the Earl of Yarborough.

SANDOWN — Mostly Victorian in design. Worth a visit is the Geological Museum in nearby Wilkes Road.

WHITE CLIFF BAY

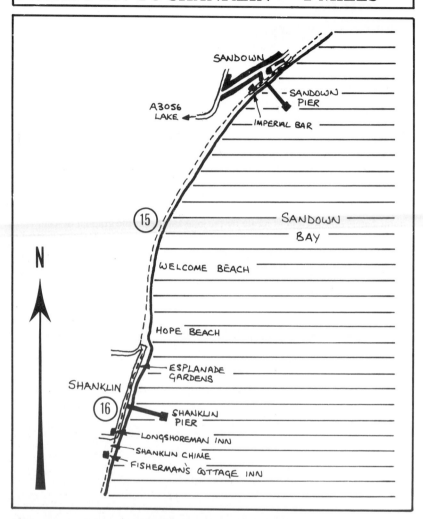

SANDOWN

A3056 LAKE

SANDOWN PIER

IMPERIAL BAR

N

(15)

SANDOWN BAY

WELCOME BEACH

HOPE BEACH

ESPLANADE GARDENS

SHANKLIN

(16)

SHANKLIN PIER

LONGSHOREMAN INN

SHANKLIN CHINE

FISHERMAN'S COTTAGE INN

SANDOWN

SANDOWN PIER TO SHANKLIN PIER — 2 MILES
- allow 50 minutes.

ABOUT THE SECTION — The most built up section of the walk as you link two of the island's principal holiday areas together. You walk along the concrete wall above the beach and groynes.

WALKING INSTRUCTIONS — From Sandown Pier continue along the Esplanade past the Imperial Bar and onto the concrete walkway and keep on this for the next 1½ miles to the road at Shanklin. Gaining it, turn left to keep close to the shoreline as you walk along Esplanade Gardens to reach Shanklin Pier.

SHANKLIN — Major tourist resort but the Old Village of Shanklin with its thatched houses is worth a visit. During the summer months Shanklin Chine can be explored on payment of a small admission charge. The sandstone gorge was a haunt for smugglers, contains numerous plants, has impressive waterfalls and is floodlit at night.

SHANKLIN PIER

13

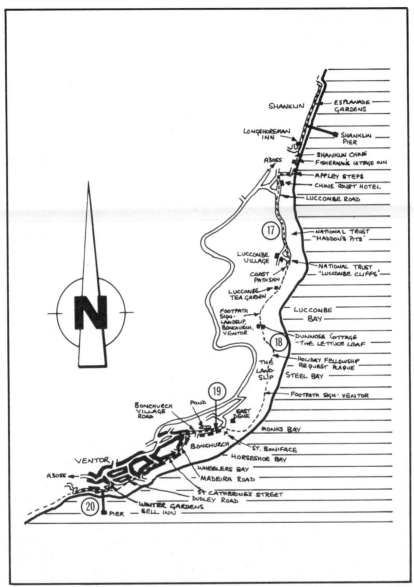

SHANKLIN

ESPLANADE GARDENS

LONGSHOREMAN INN

SHANKLIN PIER

A3055

SHANKLIN CHINE
FISHERMAN'S COTTAGE INN

APPLEY STEPS

CHINE COURT HOTEL

LUCCOMBE ROAD

17

NATIONAL TRUST "HADDON'S PITS"

LUCCOMBE VILLAGE

COAST PATH SIGN

NATIONAL TRUST "LUCCOMBE CLIFFS"

LUCCOMBE TEA GARDEN

FOOTPATH SIGN - LANDSLIP, BONCHURCH, VENTNOR

LUCCOMBE BAY

18

DUNNOSE COTTAGE - THE LETTUCE LEAF

HOLIDAY FELLOWSHIP REQUEST PLAQUE

THE LAND-SLIP

STEEL BAY

FOOTPATH SIGN - VENTNOR

19

POND

BONCHURCH VILLAGE ROAD

EAST DENE

MONKS BAY

BONCHURCH

ST. BONIFACE

HORSESHOE BAY

VENTNOR

WHEELERS BAY

A3055

MADEIRA ROAD

ST CATHERINE'S STREET
DUDLEY ROAD

20

PIER

WINTER GARDENS
BELL INN

ST. BONIFACE CHURCH — dates from Norman times and dedicated in 1070 A.D. The church is just over 48 feet long and 12 feet wide.

VENTNOR — Mostly Victorian and was largely developed by the physician, Sir James Clark, in the 1830's who described the area as "The English Madeira." St. Boniface Down, National Trust property, is the highest point on the island at 787 feet. Close to Ventnor are the Botanic Gardens covering 22 acres. Adjacent is the Museum of Smuggling History, illustrating 700 years of worldwide smuggling methods.

SHANKLIN PIER TO VENTNOR PIER — 4 MILES
- allow 2 hours.

ABOUT THE SECTION — A remarkably varied section full of surprises and some of the finest walking on the whole route. First you pass the renowned Shanklin Chine and beautifully thatched Fisherman's Cottage Inn, before ascending to the cliff tops and on towards Luccombe with further thatched buildings and outstanding area, The Landslip. Next you approach the 11th century St. Boniface Church before weaving your way down to Ventnor and its pier.

WALKING INSTRUCTIONS — From the pier continue along the Esplanade past the Longshoreman Inn and on close to the shore to the entrance to Shanklin Chine and Fisherman's Cottage Inn. Continue beside the shore for another 100 yards before leaving it and ascending the Appley Steps . At the top walk round the Chine Court Hotel to your left into Luccombe Road. Keep on this road heading towards Luccombe Village for ½ mile. Where the road turns right to the village keep ahead, first on a road then path as you enter Luccombe Cliffs, National Trust property. The path soon becomes a lane as you keep ahead past the thatched Luccombe Tea Garden. ¼ mile later gain a footpath sign — Landslip, Bonchurch and Ventnor. The coast path is signed to Nansen Hill but for me you miss one of the finest parts of the walk. By following my route you rejoin the "true Coast Path" on the Down above St. Lawrence 4 miles away. You continue on the tarmaced surface past another thatched Tea Room, then Dunnose Cottage — the Lettuce Leaf — and ¼ mile later the entrance to the Landslip, beside a Holiday Fellowship Request plaque.

"Friend, when you stray, or sit and
take your ease
On moor, or fell or under spreading trees
Pray, leave no trace of your wayside meal
No paper bag, no scattered orange peel;
nor Daily Journal littered on the grass,
others may view these with distaste, and pass.
Let no one say, and say it to your shame,
that all was beauty here until you came."

Follow the path through the woodland of the Landslip, after ½ mile passing a Ventnor path sign, and ¼ mile further Monks Bay Cottage. Just after it becomes a fenced path and to your right is East Dene. At the end of the path reach St. Boniface Church and turn right to the main road — Bonchurch Village Road. Turn left along it past the Huish Memorial Grotto and pond on your right. Shortly afterwards take the first road on your left — Madeira Road — which ascends and doubles back on you before passing above Wheelers Bay and past Ventnor Towers Hotel. Keep ahead at all road junctions into St. Catherine's Street, then Dudley Road and car park. Just after bear left at path sign — East Cliff — and pass the viewing circle showing St. Catherines Lighthouse is 4 miles away. Descend to the waterfall and switchback road at Ventnor just before the pier.

LANDSLIP, Nr. Luccombe — Because of the geological makeup of the area, the ground is unstable and slowly slipping. A major landslip occurred in 1810 and another in 1928. Despite this the wooded area is one of the finest places on the island.

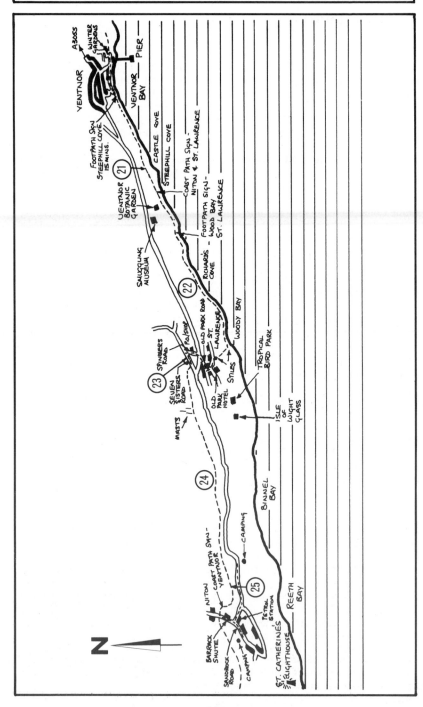

VENTNOR PIER TO ST. CATHERINE'S (NITON) — 5½ MILES
- allow 2½ hours

ABOUT THE SECTION — The first half keeps you along the coastline to St. Lawrence. Just inland is Ventnor Botanic Gardens and Museum of Smuggling History, which being so close are well worth vsiting. From St. Lawrence you leave the coast and ascend inland and walk high up along the tops of woodlined cliffs to the southern edge of Niton, with St. Catherine's lighthouse ½ mile away.

WALKING INSTRUCTIONS — From Ventnor Pier continue along Pier Street past the shops to the path sign — Steephill Cove, 15 minutes. Keep close to the shoreline on the tarmaced path and after ½ mile ascend some steps to be above Steephill Cove. Keep to the edge of the cliffs on the path, as footpath signed — St. Lawrence and Niton. Shorlty afterwards pass Ventnor Botanic Gardens on your right and almost immediately afterwards, the Smuggling Museum. Continue along the tops passing more path signs — Woody Bay and St, Lawrence. In another mile reach Woody Bay and a stile. Here turn right at the path sign — St. Lawrence — and leave the coastline. After a few yards leave the track and keep the field boundary on your left to reach another stile followed by a kissing gate. Turn left along the road and near the Old Park Hotel turn right along the road — Old Park Road — and bear right again shortly afterwards to reach the main road — A3055 — in St. Lawrence, near the St. Lawrence Inn.

Cross the road and walk up Spindlers Road, passing the shop and Post Office on your right. At the top turn left along Seven Sisters Road, and 50 yards later at the footpath sign turn right and ascend to the top of the cliffs and path sign — Niton. Turn left and keep to the path close to the wooded edge on your left. First you pass masts and approximately 1½ miles later you curve round and descend to the main road — A3055 — at the southern edge of Niton. The coast path continues opposite but to your left are two campsites; one just beside the A3055 road and another via Barrack Shute and Sandrock Road. The area is well worth exploring with St. Catherine's Lighthouse and Point nearby, the southernmost point of the island.

ST. LAWRENCE — named after Lawrence, Archdeacon of Rome, who died in 258 A.D. In the Old Park is a Tropical Bird Park with walk-through aviaries and a glass works.

ST CATHERINE'S LIGHTHOUSE — Built in 1840 and stands 84 feet tall. The light is 5¼ million candle power and is visible 18 miles away.

VENTNOR BAY

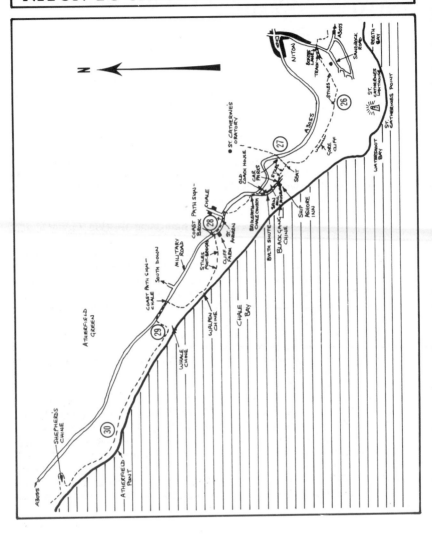

ST. CATHERINE'S ORATORY — A mediaeval lighthouse built in about 1320 by Walter de Bodyton and because of its octagonal shape often referred to as the "Pepper Pot."

BLACKGANG CHINE — Former haunt of smugglers but now a major theme park. The park was orginally opened in 1843 and is now a principal tourist attraction of southern England. The views of the coast and its erosion are particularly attractive. Opposite is Blackgang Sawmill, a replica of a Victorian water-powered sawmill, with displays of associate industries including wheelwright and cooperage.

ST. CATHERINE'S (NITON) TO SHEPHERD'S CHINE — 5 MILES
- allow 2½ hours.

ABOUT THE SECTION — For just over a mile you continue the high level walk well away from the shore, before entering Blackgang and its amusement area. Another place to explore, if time permits, with an inn, and ½ mile inland St. Catherine's Oratory. A further ½ mile brings you to Chale where you return to the cliff tops to set the theme for the walk to the Needles, 12 miles away. The cliffs are badly eroded due to soft composition and you will have to frequently walk around "Chines" — these are deep ravines. It is interesting to note the various names these ravines are called in different parts of the country; in the Orkneys and Shetlands they are called, Geo's.

WALKING INSTRUCTIONS — From the road on the southern edge of Niton, cross the road into Boyers Lane, a track. You soon reach a stile and continue along the field edge with the cliff edge on your left. ½ mile later you walk along the top of Gore Cliff with its exposed rock faces. ¼ mile later you reach a seat and fenced path on your right. This leads to a car park and path to St. Catherine's Oratory. Bear left and descend steeply to a stile and enter the main car park of Blackgang. Keep ahead past the Ship Ashore Inn, Saw Mill Museum and Blackgang Chine. Keep on the road past the Old Coach House to the main road — Blythe Shute. Turn left and left almost immediately by the Chale sign onto the bridleway — Chale Church. In little over ¼ mile you reach another path sign — Chale Church — and a few more yards brings you to the road in Chale. Turn left, and on your right is Chale Church dedicated to St. Andrew.

Continue along the road — Military Road — for 200 yards to the coastal path sign — Brook — just past Cliff Farm. Turn left over the stile and follow the defined path along the field edge to another stile and footbridge. Ahead can be seen another sign, and once here you bear right along the cliff tops of Chale Bay. After ½ mile and as indicated by a sign you leave the coast and walk to your right to the road. Turn left along it to a car park and just after left, as coastal path signed, and return to the cliff tops. The detour is caused by Whale Chine; one of many detours on this stretch of coast. Back on the cliff tops you continue close to the edge for the next two miles to Shepherd's Chine. Here a path loops round the Chine, but another with steps and footbridge goes straight ahead to coastal path sign — Chale 3 miles, Freshwater Bay 8 miles, and Brook 4½ miles.

BOATS NEAR ATHERFIELD ROCKS

19

SHEPERD'S CHINE TO MARSH CHINE — 3 MILES

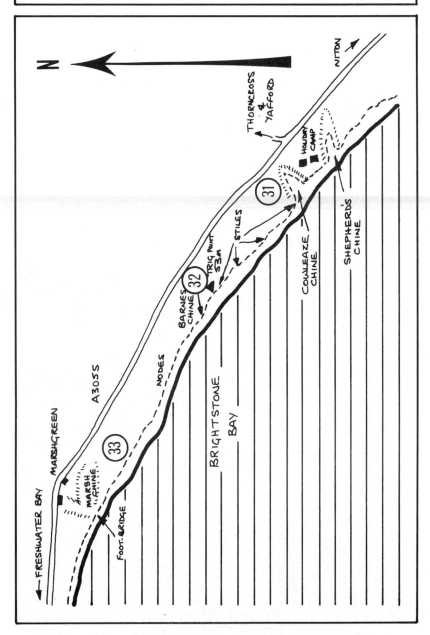

SHEPHERD'S CHINE TO MARSH CHINE — 3 MILES
- allow 1¼ hours.

ABOUT THE SECTION — After detouring around Cowleaze Chine you keep along the cliff tops of Brightstone Bay all the way to Marsh Chine. There are no amenities on this section and none will be passed until Freshwater, 8 miles ahead.

WALKING INSTRUCTIONS — From the coastal path sign on the northern edge of Shepherd's Chine, walk past the holiday camp and after ¼ mile walk around Cowleaze Chine and regain the cliff tops. For the next 2½ miles you keep close to the edge, following a sometimes faint path, but one that is well stiled. After ¾ mile pass Trig Point 53 metres and in almost two miles gain Marsh Chine. En route there are two side paths but ignore these. Descend to the footbridge over the stream in Marsh Chine and gain the coastal path sign — Brook.

FRESHWATER BAY SIGN

ST. BONIFACE CHURCH

21

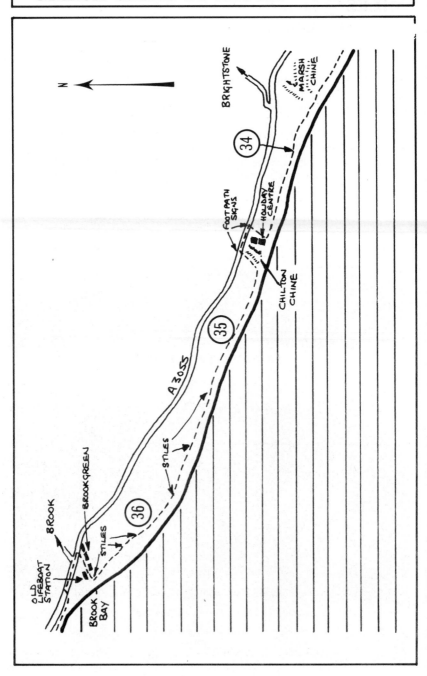

MARSH CHINE TO BROOK — 3 MILES
- allow 1¼ hours.

ABOUT THE SECTION — Only one detour around Chilton Chine, otherwise it is cliff walking all the way to Brook and its old Lifeboat Station.

WALKING INSTRUCTIONS — From Marsh Chine continue along the cliff tops past the campsite of Grange Farm and in ¾ mile turn right to the main road, A3055. This is so you walk around a Holiday Centre and Chilton Chine. Turn left at the road beside the footpath sign and, 125 yards later, left at the next footpath sign and walk above the western edge of Chilton Chine and regain the cliff tops, where you bear right. For the next two miles you keep on the cliff tops on a well stiled path to Brookgreen and its old lifeboat station.

OLD LIFEBOAT STATION, BROOK

OLD LIFEBOAT HOUSE, BROOK — The lifeboat in the 19th century was taken to and from the sea by eight horses and oared against the tide to the rescue. The stories of their heroism and dedication to such perilous rescues is well worth learning about. Brook Church has the lifeboat memorials.

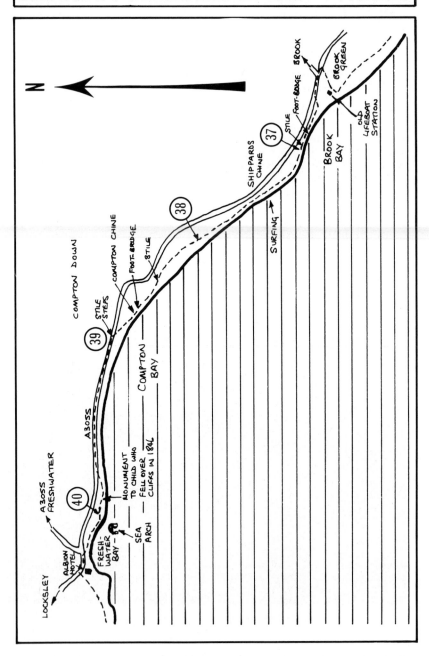

FRESHWATER BAY — The thatched church dedicated to St. Agnes was built in 1908. The chalk archway and nearby rocks known as Stag Rocks are associated with a legend that a hunted stag jumped off the cliffs onto them.

BROOK TO FRESHWATER BAY — 4 MILES
- allow 1½ hours.

ABOUT THE SECTION — You leave the soft cliffs behind and enter the imposing chalk cliffs around Compton Bay that eventually lead to The Needles. The walking is impressive and the houses of Freshwater Bay are a delightful end to this stage with full amenities.

WALKING INSTRUCTIONS — From the Old Lifeboat Station walk to the main road — A3055 — and turn left and a few yards later at the car park, left at the stile and return to the cliffs above Brook Bay. Little over ½ mile later reach Shippards Chine and car park. Keep ahead on the cliff tops. On your left is Compton Bay, a popular surfing area. For the next 1¼ miles you keep close to the cliff edge as you gently ascend to the road beneath Compton Down, reached via a stile and steps beside a path sign — Brook 2 miles, Freshwater Bay 1 mile. The path is beside the road as you walk above the steep Freshwater Cliff for ¾ mile.

Then you can leave the road side and regain the cliff tops on a good path and pass a sad monument to a person who fell over the cliffs here on August 28th 1846. Shortly after below you on your left is a magnificent rock archway. A little later descend steps and enter Freshwater Bay to the prominent Albion Hotel.

YARMOUTH MARINA

FRESHWATER BAY TO THE NEEDLES— 3½ MILES

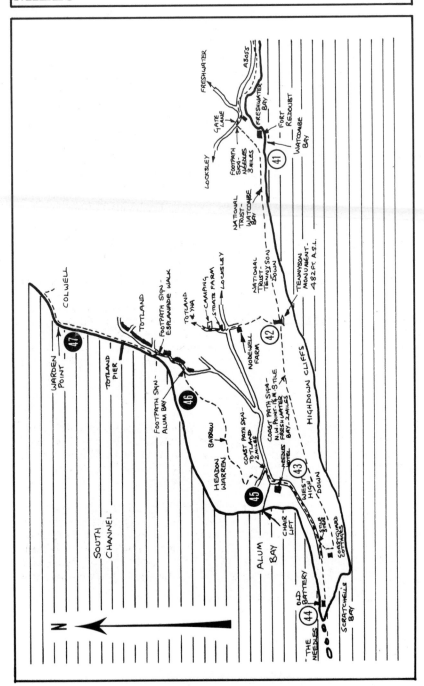

FRESHWATER BAY TO THE NEEDLES — 3½ MILES
- allow 1½ hours.

ABOUT THE SECTION — A magnificent walk over Tennyson Down and West High Down to the impressive Needles. Views abound as you gently ascend the lush grass of the down to Tennyson's Monument — 147 metres (482 feet) above sea level. From the monument, a path leads northwards down to Nodewell where there is a campsite and an inn; the Totland Youth Hostel is a further ½ mile away. A section of the walk to savour for its stunning coastal scenery.

WALKING INSTRUCTIONS — Bear right past the Albion Inn along Gate Lane for a few yards to the footpath sign — The Needles, 3 miles — on your left. Turn left along the track with Fort Redoubt on your left. In ¼ mile you look down on Watcombe Bay and bearing right you begin ascending, gradually, up the Down towards Tennyson's Monument, 1½ miles away. The pathline is not defined, being open country. On your left are the cliffs and soon the monument appears ahead guiding you up the Down. At the monument you can turn right and descend to the campsite at Stoats Farm and the Youth Hostel further away.

From the monument the path now descends away from the cliffs and in ½ mile you reach a stile and coastal path sign — Westernmost Point — 1¼ miles and Freshwater Bay — 2 miles. Go over the stile and now begin ascending over West High Down. In a little over ½ mile you begin to descend with the coastguard cottages ahead. Turn right in front of the buildings to reach a stile, steps and track. By following this to your left you reach incomparable views of The Needles and Needles Old Battery, National Trust property. The track to your right leads to Alum Bay and its Chair Lift.

TENNYSON DOWN AND MONUMENT — The downs, National Trust property are an exceptional vantage point over the channel. The chalk down has a very interesting plant life; of particular note are its orchids. The downs are crowned at their high point, 482 feet, by a monument to Lord Tennyson. He lived at Farringford House, nearby, from 1853 for many years.

THE NEEDLES — Spectacular fins of chalk with a red painted lighthouse at the end, guarding the western entrance to The Solent. The lighthouse was built in 1859 and is 109 feet high. The cliffs are home to a wide range of sea birds during the summer months. The Needles Battery; National Trust property, is open during the warmer months and was built in 1862. An exhibition on the Needles Headland can be seen plus a walk along a 200 foot tunnel providing stunning views of the Needles.

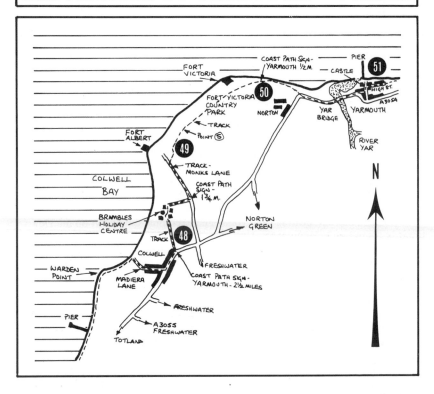

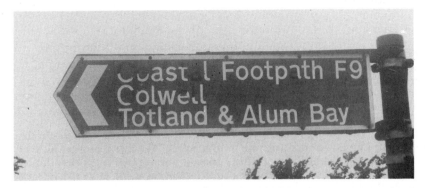

TOTLAND PATH SIGN

ALUM BAY — Takes name from Alum ore that was mined nearby as early as 1562. The bay is reached by chair lift and the cliffs are fascinating being banded by more than 20 different colours, from brown to pink.

TOTLAND — Takes its name from Tootland, meaning a lookout. A beacon is known to have existed on the summit of Headon Warren.

THE NEEDLES TO YARMOUTH — 7 MILES
- allow 2½ hours.

ABOUT THE SECTION — A remarkably contrasting walk as you begin walking the north western shoreline of the island. Leaving the impressive cliffs of Alum Bay and The Needles behind you, cross heather moorland before regaining the shoreline on the Esplanade of Freshwater. A mile later you walk inland through Colwell and around a Holiday Centre before walking through woodland near Fort Victoria Country Park. Shortly after you are back beside the sea as you approach Yarmouth and cross Yar Bridge.

WALKING INSTRUCTIONS — From the stile and steps below the Coastguard Cottages, turn right along the track above the White Cliffs. After ½ mile bear left down the road at Largesse (Garden Gnomes) to reach the amusement centre of Alum Bay, passing the Glass works, Needles Hotel, and chair lift. Follow the road (B3322) round to your right for 100 yards to the track and coastal path sign — Totland, 2 miles. 50 yards along here turn right at the kissing gate and enter Headon Warren. The path is defined as you ascend to a vantage point on your left, where you turn right and ascend to the summit of the heather clad Headon Hill complete with Barrow. Shortly afterwards you turn left and descend a defined path/track and at a seat keep on the left track which soon becomes a path; in just over ¼ mile reach a minor road beside the footpath sign — Alum Bay. Turn left and ¼ mile later left at the footpath sign — Esplanade Walk — and descend to the shore beside the Freshwater Lifeboat Station used between 1885-1924. Bear right along the esplanade to the pier.

Continue on past the pier along the Esplanade and in ½ mile walk round Warden Point. Continue past another Holiday Centre and just past Colwell Chine leave the coast and walk into Colwell along Madeira Lane. Just over ¼ mile reach the A3054 road beside a footpath sign. Turn left and ¼ mile later left at the coastal path sign — Yarmouth 2½ miles. Follow the track past Brambles Farm and into Brambles Holiday Centre. The pathline is well signed here as you turn right, then left, then right along a track to Monk"s Lane. All the coastal path signs indicate the route to Yarmouth via Fort Victoria Country Park. A further ¼ mile and you leave the track at a stile on your right and soon walk past an old Battery and reach Point 5 on an information trail. Continue on a track, now in woodland, and in¾ mile gain the minor road with Fort Victoria on your left. Just ahead is the coastal path sign — Yarmouth ½ mile. You are now close to the shore again as you walk round to the main road — A3054. Turn left along the road over Yar Bridge into Yarmouth. Where the main road turns right keep ahead past the Wheatsheaf Inn and turn left in the main shopping area then right into High Street.

FORT ALBERT AND VICTORIA — Built in the 1840's as part of the defence of The Solent, but their guns never fired on any enemy. Fort Victoria has been converted to a Country Park.

YARMOUTH — Granted a charter as a Borough in 1135. The church, dedicated to St. James, was built in the 1620's but was burnt down twice and restored in 1873. The Town Hall was rebuilt in 1763 and the castle in 1547. The latter was manned until 1975. The harbour is one of the deepest on the island and the home of the Royal Solent Yatch Club.

YARMOUTH TO SHALFLEET — 8 MILES

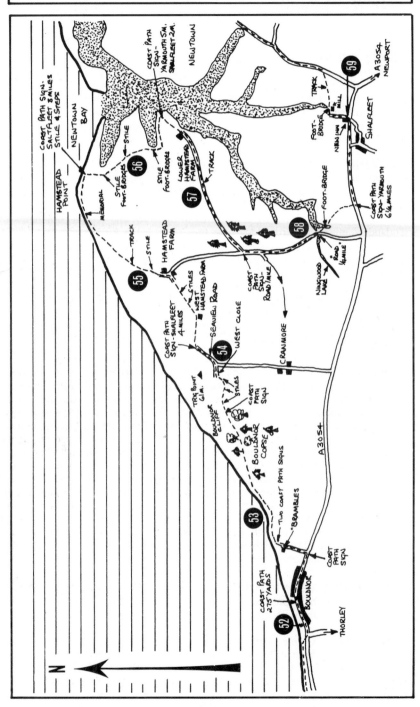

YARMOUTH TO SHALFLEET — 8 MILES
- allow 3¼ hours.

ABOUT THE SECTION — A committing and remote section as there are no facilities along the route until you get to Shalfleet. The first shop is not for almost twelve miles at Porchfield. Although you only move eastwards five miles you walk nearly twice as far as you walk round the Hamstead peninsula and round the arms of Newtown River. Again it is magnificent walking partly through forest and beside sea and estuary with abundant wildlife.

WALKING INSTRUCTIONS — Continue along the High Street out of Yarmouth, when you can return to the shoreline for ¼ mile before joining the A3054 road. Bear left along it through the village of Bouldnor. The coastal path is signed and after ½ mile of road walking turn left and walk down the lane to "Brambles" house on your left. On your right is a coast path sign and the footpath, which at first keeps near the shore on the edge of Bouldnor Copse; Forestry Commission. After little over ¼ mile you move away from the shore and gently ascend through the forest above Bouldnor Cliff and in ½ mile reach a coastal path sign — Yarmouth 2 miles; Shalfleet. Here you bear right to a stile. Continue ahead to another then left to another beside a coast path sign. Turn right along the track — West Close — and soon bear left as indicated by the coast path sign — Saltfleet 4½ miles. The mileage on the signs in this area are VERY underestimated!

Walk along Seaview Road and turn right at the bottom, at the coastal footpath sign — Saltfleet 4 miles. It is not even ¼ mile from the last sign! The path is well stiled as you walk round West Hamstead Farm and on to Hamstead. Here is another coastal path sign — Lower Hampstead. Keep on the track on the left of Hamstead Farm and start descending to the shore little over ½ mile away. Ahead are views of The Solent. Reach the shore and soon pass a monument on your right, near Hamstead Point. ¼ mile later turn right away from the shore to a stile and steps, at the coastal sign — Saltfleet 3 miles — (nearer 4½ miles!). The path is well defined across the stiled fields and footbridges. In ½ mile reach a side estuary of the Newtown River and walk around it before reaching Lower Hamstead Farm.

You now follow a track away from the estuary and in ¾ mile reach a T junction with coast path sign — Road 1 mile, Yarmouth 5 ½ miles. Turn left and in ½ mile cross the road bridge over Ningwood Lake. Almost immediately afterwards turn left at the coast path sign — Road ¼ mile. Soon cross a footbridge over an arm of the lake and bear right up the field and reach the road — A3054. Turn left and reach Shalfleet in ½ mile. Turn left at the New Inn.

SHALFLEET — The church dates from the 12th century and has 5 foot thick walls.

SHALFLEET TO PORCHFIELD — 3½ MILES

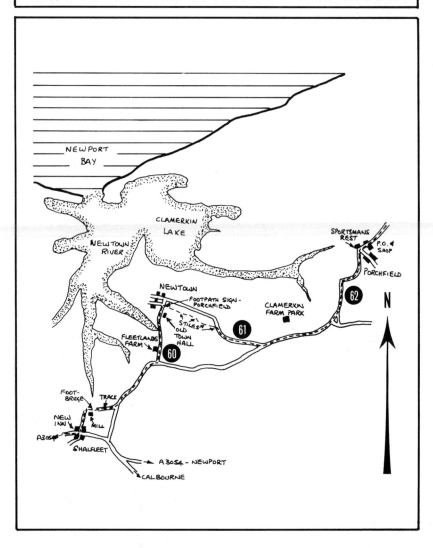

NEWTOWN — The oldest town on the island and in the 17th century a major port with more than 50 ships of 500 or more tons. Oyster fishing was the main produce and they are still being reared today. With the silting of the river the port declined and is now a major nature reserve. The Old Town Hall; National Trust property, was built in 1699 and houses a fascinating collection of documents tracing the history to the town.

SHALFLEET TO PORCHFIELD POST OFFICE — 3½ MILES
- allow 1½ hours.

ABOUT THE SECTION — You are now well away from the sea as you mostly road walk to the fascinating village of Newtown. Exploring the area is extremely interesting and one of the surprises of the whole walk. Apart from a short section across fields it is all road walking to Porchfield as you walk around a Danger Area. Porchfield has a well stocked shop and an inn.

WALKING INSTRUCTIONS — From Shalfleet walk along the minor road from the New Inn and at the car park turn right past the mill, over a footbridge and onto a track. Follow this to a minor road. Turn left along it and after ½ mile left at the next junction to gain Newtown. Walk past the Town Hall (National Trust property). A few yards later leave the road on the footpath signed — Porchfield. Basically you keep ahead across the fields on a faint path but one that is well stiled. In ½ mile reach the minor road and turn right. ½ mile later at the road junction left again for Porchfield, little over a mile away. En route pass Clamerkin Farm Park on your left. Keep on the minor road to Porchfield and its Sportsmans Rest Inn and Post Office and shop on your right.

NEWTOWN — TOWN HALL

PORCHFIELD TO GREAT THORNESS – 1½ MILES

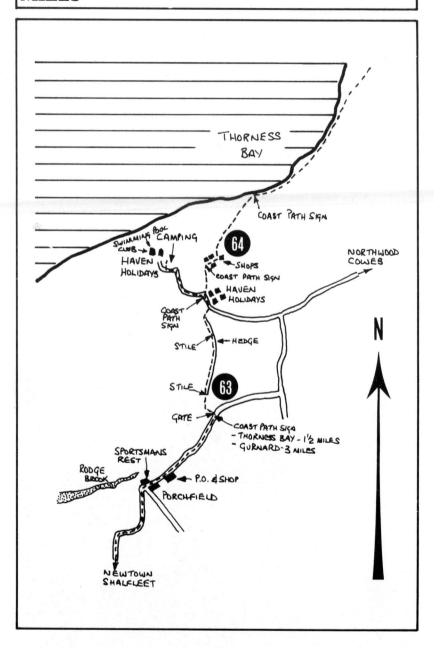

THORNESS BAY

COAST PATH SIGN

SWIMMING POOL CLUB → CAMPING

HAVEN HOLIDAYS

64

→ SHOPS

COAST PATH SIGN

HAVEN HOLIDAYS

NORTHWOOD COWES →

COAST PATH SIGN

STILE ← HEDGE

STILE

63

GATE

COAST PATH SIGN
- THORNESS BAY - 1½ MILES
- GURNARD - 3 MILES

N

SPORTSMANS REST

RODGE BROOK

← P.O. & SHOP

PORCHFIELD

NEWTOWN SHALFLEET

PORCHFIELD (POST OFFICE) TO GREAT THORNESS (HAVEN HOLIDAYS) — 1½ MILES.
- allow ½ an hour.

ABOUT THE SECTION — One of the shortest, but as this is the first campsite on the route since Totland it is an important staging post, with luxurious facilities, including shops, inn, club, and swimming pools. And, a stunning view from the campground of Thorness Bay, which you walk round soon!

WALKING INSTRUCTIONS — Continue along the road from the Post Office, ascending gently for ½ mile to the coastal path sign — Thorness Bay 1½ miles; Gurnard 3 miles. Basically keep the field boundary on your right as you head towards Great Thorness, across the well stiled fields. In just over ½ mile reach the minor road opposite Haven Holidays. Turn left and very soon on your right is the coast path sign marking the defined and well signed path through the resort to Thorness Bay. If you are planning on camping here keep on the road to your left to the reception office. You can from the site simply walk to the shop area where you will pick up the coast path to Thorness Bay.

CAMP — GREAT THORNESS

GREAT THORNESS TO COWES — 5 MILES

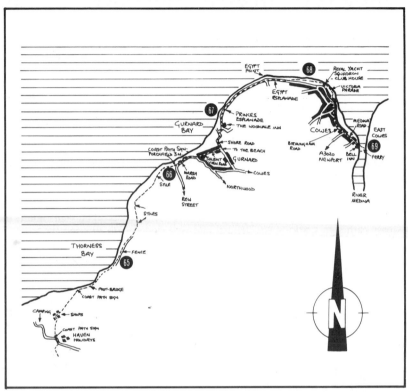

THORNESS BAY

GREAT THORNESS TO COWES (RIVER MEDINA) — 5 MILES
- allow 2¼ hours.

ABOUT THE SECTION — First you descend to the shore of Thorness Bay, the last unspoilt piece of coastline before Ryde. A cliff walk brings you to Gurnard Bay where you walk along the promenades into Cowes. The section ends at the ferry across the River Medina. The section also marks the return to "civilisation"!

WALKING INSTRUCTIONS — Continue through the holiday centre, guided by the coastal path signs, passing the shopping area and onto the path to the shore of Thorness Bay. Turn right along the shoreline and soon cross a footbridge. Keep to the shore for a further ¼ mile before bearing right to the fence on your right and walk beside it as you ascend above the mud cliffs. The path is defined and stiled and over the summit in ½ mile you descend along the field edge to the houses of Gurnard, gaining Marsh Road close to a coastal path sign — Porchfield 3 miles.

Turn left along Marsh Road, and after ¼ mile where the road turns right keep ahead and ascend Solent View Road. At the top turn left along Shore Road, signed — To The Beach. You descend passing the Woodvale Inn and gain Princes Esplanade — opened on July 22nd 1926 by his Royal Highness. Follow this for ½ mile beside the shore and continue ahead along Egypt Esplanade. After ¼ mile keep left on the esplanade and walk past the Royal Yacht Squadron Club House and into Victoria Parade. Follow this round to The Glope and Customs House and bear right to the shopping area and turn left. Pass the Pier View Inn and walk past the shops to the main road — A3020 — 1/4 mile away. Keep ahead along Medina Road to the Bell Inn and ferry across the River Medina.

COWES — Is synonymous with sailing and the famous Cowes Week and Fastnet yacht race. The first recorded race is 1788. Part of wall of the Royal Yatch Squadron headquaters is the remains of Henry V111th castle built here in the 1530's.

MARINA — GURNARD BAY

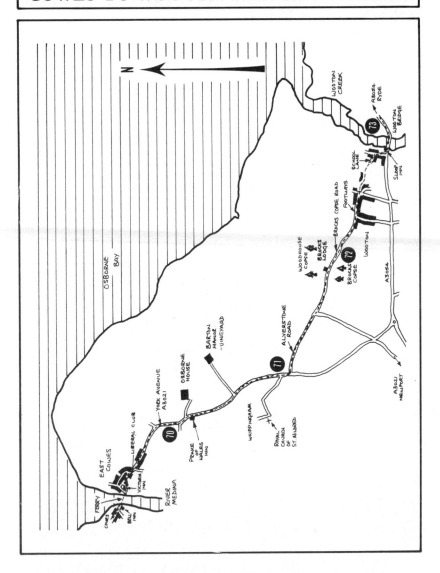

OSBORNE HOUSE — Built by Queen Victoria in 1840's in Italianate style. The grounds contain every known English tree. The house is open to the public and the apartments occupied by Queen Victoria until her death here in 1901 are on view.

BARTON MANOR VINEYARD — English vineyard with grounds laid out by Prince Albert and Queen Victoria. In Spring the woodland is covered by ¼ million daffodils. The lake has black swans and a thatched boathouse.

COWES (RIVER MEDINA) TO WOOTON BRIDGE — 4 MILES
- allow 1½ hours.

ABOUT THE SECTION — Road walking all the way, but much of it on minor roads. In the early stages you have the opportunity to visit Osborne House and the Barton Manor vineyard!

WALKING INSTRUCTIONS — Take the ferry across the River Medina and continue on the main road — A3021. Pass the Victoria Inn almost immediately, then the Liberal Club as you begin ascending out of East Cowes. Keep on the main road, York Avenue, for almost 2 miles, passing the entrance to Osborne House, then the Prince of Wales Inn on your right, and ½ mile later the entrance to Baron Manor Vineyard. ½ mile later pass Beatrice Avenue and sign for the Royal Church of St Mildred on your right. Just afterwards turn left along Alverstone Road. After ½ mile at the cross roads, keep straight ahead along Brocks Copse Road, passing Brocks Lodge, and in just over ½ mile reach Wooton. Turn left then right along Footways as you descend through the houses of Wooton. At the bottom on the left of Rectory Cottage is the footpath sign and path. Basically you keep straight ahead on a path between the houses, along Red Road. The path runs into School Lane and at the end turn right then left onto a path beside Rint Dene and reach the Stoop Inn and A3054 road. Turn left over the bridge over Wooton Creek.

COWES-E.COWES FERRY ACROSS THE RIVER MEDINA

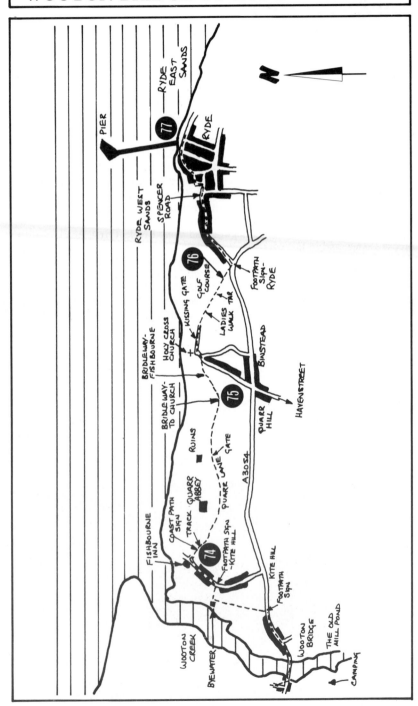

WOOTON BRIDGE TO RYDE — 4 MILES
- allow 1½ hours

ABOUT THE SECTION — The last lap! First you walk to a delightful inn and coastal views before walking along a fascinating lane past a ruined abbey. Passing a golf course you reach the outskirts of Ryde and follow a minor road back to central Ryde and its pier where you began a few days ago!

WALKING INSTRUCTIONS — Cross the road bridge and keep on the main road — A3054 — for ¼ mile. Turn left at the footpath sign — Fishbourne — and walk between the houses for 1/3 of a mile. At the house called Byewater, turn right up the fenced path. At the top turn left along the road and in ¼ mile reach the Fishbourne Inn. Just before it turn right on Quarr Lane — bridlepath signed — Binstead. For the next mile you keep on this lane/track passing Quarr Abbey on your left and a little later ruins of an earlier abbey. Little over ¼ mile later turn left at the bridlepath sign — Church Road. At the road ¼ mile later turn left to the church, dedicated to Holy Cross. Bear right in front of it to the kissing gate and onto the tarmaced path, shortly passing a sign — Ladies Walk. The hedged path passes through a golf course and in ½ mile reaches the main road — A3054.

Turn left to the footpath sign — Ryde — and walk along the road past the houses — Spencer Road. After ½ mile turn left down St. Thomas's Street. At the bottom turn right to the minor road, then left along it to Ryde's West Sands and the pier — journey's end.....alas!

QUARR ABBEY — the ruined abbey dates from 1132 with much of the stone used in coastal defences following the dissolution of the monasteries. The new abbey was completed in 1912 by a Benedictine Order of monks.

41

AMENITIES GUIDE -

Village/Town	B&B	Y.H.A.	Camp	Inn	Restaurant	Shop	P.O.
RYDE	★		★	★	★	★	★
SEAVIEW	★		★	★	★	★	★
ST. HELENS	★		★	★	★	★	★
BEMBRIDGE	★		★	★	★	★	★
CULVER DOWN				★	★		
SANDOWN	★	★		★	★	★	★
SHANKLIN	★		★	★	★	★	★
LUCCOMBE					★		
VENTNOR	★			★	★	★	★
ST. LAWRENCE				★	★	★	★
NITON	★	★	★	★	★	★	★
BLACKGANG				★	★		
ATHERFIELD			★				
MARSH GREEN			★				
FRESHWATER BAY	★			★	★		
ALUM BAY				★	★		
TOTLAND	★	★	★	★	★	★	★
YARMOUTH	★			★	★	★	★
SHALFLEET			★	★	★		★
PORCHFIELD				★		★	★
GREAT THORNESS			★	★	★	★	
COWES	★		★	★	★	★	★
WOOTON BRIDGE		★	★	★	★	★	★
FISHBOURNE				★			

INNS

- on or close to the route. Several provide accommodation as detailed.

RYDE — Redan, Union Street.
King Lud, Esplanade.
Marine Hotel, Esplanade.

SEAVIEW — Battery Hotel. Tel 712188 — accommodation.

ST. HELENS — Vine Inn.

BEMBRIDGE — Crab & Lobster. Tel 872244 — accommodation.

CULVER DOWN — Culver Haven Inn.

SANDOWN — The Tiger Tavern.
Jolly Sailor.
Royal Standard.
York Inn.

SHANKLIN — Longshoreman Inn.
Fisherman's Cottage Inn.
Crab Inn.
Plough & Barleycorn.

VENTNOR — Bonchurch Inn, Nr Ventnor. Tel. 852611 -
accommodation.
The Bell Inn.
Blenheim.

ST. LAWRENCE -St. Lawrence Inn.

NITON — Buddle Inn.
White Lion. Tel. 730293 — accommodation.

BLACKGANG — Ship Ashore Inn.

FRESHWATER
BAY — Albion Hotel.

ALUM BAY — Needles Hotel.

TOTLAND — Broadway Hotel. Tel. 752453 — accommodation.

YARMOUTH — Wheatsheaf Inn.
Bugle Hotel. Tel. 760272 — accommodation.

SHALFLEET — New Inn.

PORCHFIELD — Sportsmans Rest.

GT THORNESS — Part of Haven Holidays complex.
SS Solent Bar.

COWES — Anchor Inn, High Street.
Globe Hotel, The Parade.
Pier View Hotel, High Street. Tel.294929 -
accommodation.
Three Crowns, High Street.
Duke of York.
The Bell Inn.

EAST COWES — Victoria Inn.
Prince of Wales — opposite Osborne House.

WOOTON
BRIDGE — Sloop Inn.

FISHBOURNE — Fishbourne Inn.

FISHBOURNE INN, FISHBOURNE

YOUTH HOSTELS -

SANDOWN — The Firs, Fitzroy Street, Sandown, Isle of Wight
PO36 8JH. Tel. 0983-402651

WHITWELL — 1 mile from route at St. Lawrence.
Whitwell, Ventnor, Isle of Wight. PO38 2PP
Tel. 0983-730473

TOTLAND BAY — Hurst Hill, Summers Lane, Totland Bay,
Isle of Wight. PO39 OHD
Tel. 0983-752165

WOOTON BRIDGE — New Road, Wooton Bridge, Ryde, Isle of Wight
PO33 4HX Tel. 0983-882348
* only open mid July to end of August. Bookings
to YHA, 58 Streatham High Road, London, SW16 1DA.

BED AND BREAKFAST -

RYDE — Seaward Guest House, 14-16 George Street, Ryde PO33 2EW. Tel. 0983-63168

Mr & Mrs R. Austin, 36 George Street, Ryde, PO33 2EN. Tel. 0983-63968

SEAVIEW — The Nutshell, Fairy Road, Seaview. Tel. 713880

ST. HELENS — Duver House, Duver Road, St. Helens. Tel. 872311

BEMBRIDGE — Highbury Hotel, Lane End Road, Bembridge. Tel. 873941

SANDOWN — Mr & Mrs C. Probert, Moncoffer Guest House, 26 Melville Street, Sandown. PO36 8HX Tel. 405410

Marine Villa Guest House, 16 York Road, Sandown. PO36 8ET Tel. 405337

SHANKLIN — Mrs P. Metcalf, Culham Lodge, 31 Landguard Manor Road, Shanklin. PO37 7HZ. Tel. 862880.

Mr & Mrs Davies, Soraba Private Hotel, 2 Paddock Road, Shanklin. PO37 6NZ. Tel 862367.

VENTNOR — Hillside Hotel, 151 Mitchell Avenue, Ventnor. PO38 1DR.   Tel.   852271.

Mrs F. Rigby, Rock Cottage, Belgrave Road, Ventnor. PO38 1JD. Tel. 855105.

NITON — Puckmaster Lodge Hotel, St. Catherine's Road, Niton. Tel. 730649.

**FRESHWATER
BAY** — Saunders Hotel, Coastguard Lane, Freshwater Bay. PO40 9QX Tel. 0983-752322.

TOTLAND BAY — Mrs R Padwick, Almonte, 55 The Avenue, Totland Bay. PO39 0DN. Tel. 0983-752028.

The Nodes Country Hotel, Alum Bay Old Road, Totland Bay. PO39 0HZ. Tel. 0983-752859.

YARMOUTH — Mrs J Manfield, St Hilda, Victoria Road, Yarmouth. PO41 1QW. Tel. 760814.

Quinces, Cranmore Avenue, Yarmouth.
Tel. 760080.

COWES — Grantham Hotel, Queens Road, Cowes.
Tel. 0983-293380.

Caledon Guest House, 59 Mill Hill Road, Cowes.
PO31 7EG. Tel. 293599.

CAMPING SITES -

RYDE — Both sites are approximately 2 miles south of Ryde
close to the A3055 road.

Mrs D Faithfull, Barnsley Farm Camping Park,
The Cottage, Bullen Road, Ryde. Tel. 0983-62475

Mrs K M Paul, Beaper Farm Camping Site, Beaper Farm
Nr Ryde. Tel.0983-615210.

SEAVIEW — Pondwell Camping Holidays, Seaview, Nr. Ryde.
Tel. 0983-612330.

ST. HELENS — Mrs M Lovegrove, Carpenters Farm, St. Helens.
Tel. 0983-872450.

Mrs Bowen, Guildford Park Holiday Camping Site,
St. Helens. Tel. 0983-872821.

BEMBRIDGE — Whitecliff Bay Holiday Park, Whitecliff Bay,
Bembridge. Tel. 0983-872671.

SHANKLIN — A F J Welti, Landguard Camping Park, Landguard
Manor Road, Shanklin. Tel. 0983-863100.

NITON — Undercliff Riviera Holiday Park, Niton Undercliff.
Tel. 0983-730268.

ATHERFIELD — Mrs H Goody, Chine Farm Camping Site, Military Rd,
Atherfield. Tel. 0983-740228.

TOTLAND — Stoats Farm.

SHALFLEET — At Newbridge; 1 mile south of route from Shalfleet.
The Orchards Holiday Caravan Park, Newbridge.
Tel. 0983-78331.

GREAT
THORNESS — Haven Holidays, Thorness Bay Holiday Park.

EAST COWES — Waverley Park, Old Road, East Cowes.
Tel. 0983-293452.

WOOTON
BRIDGE — Lakeside Holiday Park, Wooton Bridge.
Tel. 0983-882530.

COAST PATH SIGN — BLUE WITH WHITE LETTERS

WILD FLOWERS — a random list.

Sea Thrift
Red Campion
Sea Mallow
Pyramid Orchid
Yellow Sea Poppy
Clover
Spotted Heath Orchid
Honeysuckle
Sea Holly
Kidney Vetch
Wild Carrot
Ragwort
Hardheads
Yellow Loosestrife
Dog Rose
Sea Lavender
Sea Purslane
Spring Squill
Dog Violet
Long Leaved Scurvy Grass
Bird's-Foot Trefoil
Sea Pea
Yellow Vetch
Wall Pepper
Sea Bindweed
Sea Campion

BIRDS — a random list
- some of the birds I saw on my walk.

Mute Swan
Shelduck
Grey Heron
Wren
Black Headed Gull
Fulmar
Black Backed Gull
Pheasant
Red Grouse
Cormorant
Oyster Catcher
Common Tern
Herring Gull
Jay
Nightingale
Curlew
Dunlin
Ringed Plover
Swallow
Kingfisher
Peewit
Pied Wagtail
Greater Spotted Woodpecker
Green Woodpecker
Guillemot
Kittiwake
Magpie

SWAN AND CYGNET, WOOTON BRIDGE

EQUIPMENT NOTES — some personal thoughts

BOOTS — preferably with a full leather upper, of medium weight, with a vibram sole. I always add a foam cushioned insole to help cushion the base of my feet.

SOCKS — I generally wear two thick pairs as this helps minimise blisters. The inner pair are of loop stitch variety and approximately 80% wool. The outer are a thick rib pair of approximately 80% wool.

WATERPROOFS — for general walking I wear a T shirt or shirt with a cotton wind jacket on top. You generate heat as you walk and I prefer to layer my clothes to avoid getting too hot. Depending on the season will dictate how many layers you wear. In soft rain I just use my wind jacket for I know it quickly dries out. In heavy downpours I slip on a neoprene lined cagoule, and although hot and clammy it does keep me reasonably dry. Only in extreme conditions will I don overtrousers, much preferring to get wet and feel comfortable.

FOOD — as I walk I carry bars of chocolate, for they provide instant energy and are light to carry. In winter a flask of hot coffee is welcome. I never carry water and find no hardship from doing so, but this is a personal matter! From experience I find the more I drink the more I want and sweat. You should always carry some extra food such as Kendal mint cake, for emergencies.

RUCKSACKS — for day walking I use a climbing rucsac of about 40 litre capacity and although it leaves excess space it does mean that the sac is well padded, with an internal frame and padded shoulder straps. Inside apart from the basics for the day I carry gloves, balaclava, spare pullover and a pair of socks.

MAP & COMPASS — when I am walking I always have the relevant map — preferably the 1:25,000 scale — open in my hand. This enables me to constantly check that I am walking the right way. In case of bad weather I carry a compass, which once mastered gives you complete confidence in thick cloud or mist.

WOOTON CREEK

49

OBSERVE THE COASTAL CODE -

PLEASE DO NOT DAMAGE SALTMARSHES, SAND DUNES AND "CLIFF TOPS" BY TRAMPLING, OR MOVING ROCKS.

ALWAYS "BACK FILL" HOLES WHEN BAIT DIGGING AS THESE MAY BE A DANGER TO OTHERS.

MAKE YOUR VISIT INSTRUCTIVE BY PLANNING FIELD TRIPS CAREFULLY WITH CONSERVATION IN MIND.

TAKE PHOTOGRAPHS NOT LIVE SPECIMENS.

PLEASE DO NOT COLLECT LIVE ANIMALS OR SEAWEEDS, LEAVE THEM FOR OTHERS TO ENJOY.

THE COAST IS HOME FOR MANY PLANTS AND ANIMALS AND THEY MAY BE DESTROYED BY OUR CARELESS ACTIONS.

REMEMBER AND OBSERVE THE COUNTRY CODE

Enjoy the countryside and respect its life and work.

Guard against all risk of fire.

Fasten all gates.

Keep your dogs under close control.

Keep to public paths across farmland.

Use gates and stiles to cross fences, hedges and walls.

Leave livestock, crops and machinery alone.

Take your letter home — pack it in, pack it out.

Help to keep all water clean.

Protect wildlife, plants and trees.

Take special care on country roads.

Make no unnecessary noise.

LOG

Date Started .2nd. Sept. .... Date Completed ....

| Route Point | Mile No | Time | | Comments/ |
		Arr.	Dep.	Weather
RYDE	0	1.30	2.05	GOOD
APPLEY BEACH	1			
NETTLESTONE PT.	2½			
SEAVIEW	3			
ST. HELEN'S CHURCH	4½			
ST. HELEN'S	5			
BEMBRIDGE HARBOUR	6			
FORELAND	8			
WHITECLIFF BAY	10			
CULVER DOWN	11			
RED CLIFFS	12			
SANDOWN PIER	14			
WELCOME BEACH	15			
SHANKLIN PIER	16			
LUCCOMBE	17			
THE LANDSLIP	18			
BONCHURCH	19			
VENTNOR PIER	20			
CASTLE COVE	21			
ST. LAWRENCE	23			
NITON	25½			
ST. CATHERINES	26			
BLACKGANG	27			
BROOK	28			
WHALE CHINE	29			
SHEPHERD'S CHINE	30½			
BARNES CHINE	32			
MARSH CHINE	33½			
CHILTON CHINE	34½			
BROOKGREEN	36½			
SHIPPARDS CHINE	37½			
COMPTON DOWN	39			
FRESHWATER BAY	40½			
TENNYSON MONUMENT	42			
WEST HIGH DOWN	43			
NEEDLES OLD BATTERY	44			
ALUM BAY	45			
TOTLAND PIER	46½			
COLWELL	48			
FORT VICTORIA	50			
YARMOUTH	51			
BOULDNOR	52			
HAMSTEAD FARM	55			
LOWER HAMPSTEAD	57			
NINGWOOD LAKE	58			

SHALFLEET	59			
NEWTOWN	60½			
PORCHFIELD	62½			
THORNESS BAY	64½			
GURNARD	66			
COWES	68			
MEDINA FERRY	69			
BROCKS COPSE	72			
WOOTON BRIDGE	73			
FISHBOURNE INN	74			
BINSTEAD	75			
RYDE PIER	77			

MEMORIAL — HAMSTEAD POINT

FOOTBRIDGE — HAMSTEAD

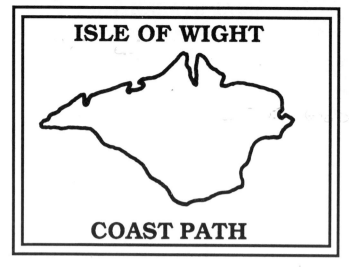

ISLE OF WIGHT

COAST PATH

Badges are navy cloth with island outline and letters embroidered in white and measure 3 1/2″ wide by 3 ″ high.

BADGE ORDER FORM

Date completed ....

Time ....

Name ....

Address ....

....

Price - £2.25 each including postage, VAT and signed certificate.

"I've done a John Merrill Walk" T shirt - Emerald Green with white lettering - all sizes - £5.50 including postage and VAT.

From - J.N.M. Publications, Winster, Matlock, Derbyshire. DE4 2DQ
☎ Winster - 062988 - 454 (24 hrs.) Fax: Winster - 062988 - 416

.... **You may photocopy this form if needed** ....

THE JOHN MERRILL WALK BADGE - walk this route twice or complete another of John Merrill's Challenge Walks and send details and cheque for £2.25 for a special circular four colour embroidered badge, to J .N.M. Publications; price includes postage and VAT.

MAP SYMBOLS

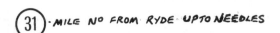 - MILE Nº FROM RYDE · UPTO NEEDLES

 - MILE Nº FROM RYDE BEYOND NEEDLES

C/P - COAST PATH SIGN

---- ROUTE

=== - SEA

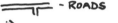 - ROADS

🌲🌳 WOODLAND

💧 - ESTUARY OR LAKE

COAST NEAR ST. LAWRENCE

NINGWOOD LAKE

OTHER BOOKS by JOHN N. MERRILL PUBLISHED by JNM PUBLICATIONS

CIRCULAR WALK GUIDES -
SHORT CIRCULAR WALKS IN THE PEAK DISTRICT
LONG CIRCULAR WALKS IN THE PEAK DISTRICT
CIRCULAR WALKS IN WESTERN PEAKLAND
SHORT CIRCULAR WALKS IN THE STAFFORDSHIRE MOORLANDS
SHORT CIRCULAR WALKS AROUND THE TOWNS & VILLAGES OF
THE PEAK DISTRICT
SHORT CIRCULAR WALKS AROUND MATLOCK
SHORT CIRCULAR WALKS IN THE DUKERIES
SHORT CIRCULAR WALKS IN SOUTH YORKSHIRE
SHORT CIRCULAR WALKS IN SOUTH DERBYSHIRE
SHORT CIRCULAR WALKS AROUND BUXTON
SHORT CIRCULAR WALKS IN THE HOPE VALLEY
40 SHORT CIRCULAR WALKS IN THE PEAK DISTRICT
CIRCULAR WALKS ON KINDER & BLEAKLOW
SHORT CIRCULAR WALKS IN SOUTH NOTTINGHAMSHIRE
SHIRT CIRCULAR WALKS IN CHESHIRE

CANAL WALKS -
VOL 1 - DERBYSHIRE & NOTTINGHAMSHIRE
VOL 2 - CHESHIRE & STAFFORDSHIRE
VOL 3 - STAFFORDSHIRE
VOL 4 - THE CHESHIRE RING
VOL 5 - LINCOLNSHIRE & NOTTINGHAMSHIRE
VOL 6 - SOUTH YORKSHIRE
VOL 7 - THE TRENT & MERSEY CANAL

JOHN MERRILL DAY CHALLENGE WALKS -
WHITE PEAK CHALLENGE WALK
DARK PEAK CHALLENGE WALK
PEAK DISTRICT END TO END WALKS
STAFFORDSHIRE MOORLANDS CHALLENGE WALK
THE LITTLE JOHN CHALLENGE WALK
YORKSHIRE DALES CHALLENGE WALK
NORTH YORKSHIRE MOORS CHALLENGE WALK
LAKELAND CHALLENGE WALK
THE RUTLAND WATER CHALLENGE WALK

INSTRUCTION & RECORD -
HIKE TO BE FIT.....STROLLING WITH JOHN
THE JOHN MERRILL WALK RECORD BOOK

MULTIPLE DAY WALKS -
THE RIVERS'S WAY
PEAK DISTRICT: HIGH LEVEL ROUTE
PEAK DISTRICT MARATHONS
THE LIMEY WAY
THE PEAKLAND WAY

COAST WALKS & NATIONAL TRAILS -
ISLE OF WIGHT COAST PATH
PEMBROKESHIRE COAST PATH
THE CLEVELAND WAY

PEAK DISTRICT HISTORICAL GUIDES -
A to Z GUIDE OF THE PEAK DISTRICT
DERBYSHIRE INNS - an A to Z guide
HALLS AND CASTLES OF THE PEAK DISTRICT & DERBYSHIRE
TOURING THE PEAK DISTRICT & DERBYSHIRE BY CAR
DERBYSHIRE FOLKLORE
PUNISHMENT IN DERBYSHIRE
CUSTOMS OF THE PEAK DISTRICT & DERBYSHIRE
WINSTER - a souvenir guide
ARKWRIGHT OF CROMFORD
TALES FROM THE MINES by Geoffrey Carr
PEAK DISTRICT PLACE NAMES by Martin Spray

JOHN MERRILL'S MAJOR WALKS -
TURN RIGHT AT LAND'S END
WITH MUSTARD ON MY BACK
TURN RIGHT AT DEATH VALLEY
EMERALD COAST WALK

COLOUR GUIDES -
THE PEAK DISTRICT.........Something to remember her by.

SKETCH BOOKS -
NORTH STAFFORDSHIRE SKETCHBOOK by John Creber
SKETCHES OF THE PEAK DISTRICT

IN PREPARATION -
LONG CIRCULAR WALKS IN STAFFORDSHIRE
SHORT CIRCULAR WALKS IN WEST YORKSHIRE
SHORT CIRCULAR WALKS IN THE YORKSHIRE DALES
SHORT CIRCULAR WALKS IN THE LAKE DISTRICT
SHORT CIRCULAR WALKS IN NORTH YORKSHIRE MOORS
SNOWDONIA CHALLENGE WALK
FOOTPATHS OF THE WORLD - Vol 1 - NORTH AMERICA
HIKING IN NEW MEXICO
☞ **Full list from JNM PUBLICATIONS, Winster, Matlock, Derbys.**

LUCCOMBE TEA GARDENS
NEAR SHANKLIN, ISLE OF WIGHT

☎ 0983 - 863116

Open everyday - April to October.
Weekends - November to March.

Coffee, light lunches, cream teas
& home made cakes.

Walking parties welcome
anytime of the year by prior arrangement.